Learn Soccer Positions, Rules and Plays in 24 Hours

Mirsad Hasic

DEDICATION

I dedicate this book to my wife.

TABLE OF CONTENTS

ACKNOWLEDGMENTS

I would like to thank my family for their support.

Intro

My intention for this book was to introduce you to the beautiful game of soccer. I didn't want this to be just another reference book with traditional jargon and boring illustrations.

The aim was to make it fun and entraining, which is why I chose to add a personal tone to the pages that follow.

Over the years I have read quite a few books on this very topic. I know by experience that a lot of them tend to have a non-personal approach.

This formal style of writing gets pretty rigid and monotonous for the reader.

As you've invested your money into this book I want you to get more than mere instruction out of it. It's important to me personally that you feel you've gotten real bang for your buck.

I want to teach you how the game actually is played in practice, and not just give theoretical pointers.

My opinion is that you only need to learn positions, rules, and basic plays, in order to understand how the game is played properly.

From that, you can take your knowledge and develop the other parts that involve ball skills, tactics, formations, and so on.

Once you grasp the basics, the question whether you will become a successful player or not depends entirely on your talent, determination and practice.

No matter what background you are from, or how advanced in your game you are, everyone will be able to benefit from this book.

Even the most experienced players and coaches will found something useful in here that could enhance their knowledge about the game of soccer.

Understanding Soccer Positions

I know from experience that positions in soccer can sometimes be difficult to understand and how it can take a while to grasp fully how each of them works in practice. Every player on the soccer field is assigned a specific position before the game, and his success rate depends on how well he plays it.

Although he is supposed to play the position allocated to him, he can in fact switch positions several times during a game, but only if the referee allows him to do so. For example, a center-full back might become a forward if a player gets injured.

Another thing you should know about soccer positions is that a player is usually only allowed to move within a specific area of the field.

For instance, a left fullback is not allowed to run to the other side where the right fullback is positioned. To do so would leave a huge gap on his side that could be taken advantage of by the opponents.

You see, the whole point of soccer positions is to create a compact and well balanced team where each player defends a specific area. Wherever a player is positioned, it is his responsibility to prevent opponents from getting through it.

A metaphor I like to use when describing soccer positions is to imagine the team as being a clock where each part must work properly and synchronize with the other parts in order to display the correct time.

I don't claim you must learn all soccer positions in micro-detail in order to understand the game of soccer. In fact, it took me several years to grasp them all and to fully understand how each of them worked in practice.

Instead, I would recommend you to use these positions as a reference each time you watch soccer either LIVE or on TV. Just remembering them won't help your game much. You need to see firsthand how they work in practice, and not just study an illustration.

Remember, soccer is a team sport, and like all team sports, its success is dependent on how well the individual players work as a group, and that means everyone has to work in coordination.

Each position in this guide is demonstrated using an image. In these images, I have placed a yellow ring around a player to highlight the position being discussed.

I just want to mention that you can study these positions in any direction you want. In fact, you can start from the very top studying the positions of offensive midfielder or from the middle with the

Winger if you like. You decide, but for this book I will be starting at the back, with the position of sweeper.

Sweeper - Maestro of the Orchestra

The positions of sweeper (SW) was not something younger teams adopted as it requires a high understanding of the game and comes with great responsibility. The acronym SW is used to illustrate the position on the field.

A sweeper is always the last line of defense.

His number one mission is to take any necessary measures to prevent opponents (sometimes unfairly if necessary) from getting past him and having a free route to the goal.

The sweeper should never complicate things by trying to dribble the ball away. Any fancy moves on his part could result in him losing the ball and giving the opponent a clear road to the goal.

As mentioned earlier, this position is probably the most responsible one on the field. By the way, a sweeper is often the captain of the team as well.

This position is sometimes referred to as "the maestro or master of the orchestra" because a sweeper's job is to conduct his team.

The sweeper position was successfully utilized by Germany during the 1970s where they totally dominated the world of soccer. They were led by the mighty Franz Beckenbauer, also known as the Kaiser, which stands for king in the German language.

Beckenbauer's ability to control the game with his calm composure, and act with great authority in both defense and offense, was true soccer art. He is considered by many to be the best player ever on this particular position.

However, another great sweeper worth mentioning is Franco Baresi who played for A.C Milan. He made a total of 82 caps for the Italian national team.

Both of these players commanded great authority on the soccer field and were born leaders; something that made them ideal for the position of sweeper.

In my opinion, younger players should not be forced to play as sweeper because it requires a lot of tactical knowledge and an ability to read the game, and they just don't have the experience.

Sadly though, this position is becoming increasingly rare and most professional soccer teams have abandoned it altogether.

Center Fullback - The Iron Rock

A center fullback is the foundation of his team. He is the player who has the huge responsibility of making the defense line synchronize so as to successfully prevent the opponents from getting through it.

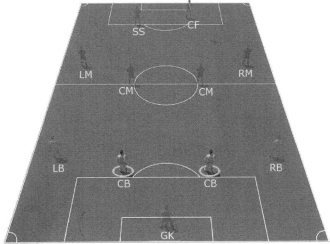

The acronym CB (center fullback) is used to illustrate the position of a center fullback.

A center fullback is located between the left and right fullback and right in front of the goalkeeper. Note how he is playing at the side of another fullback.

An ideal center back is generally a well-built player and someone who has good heading skills. He is also a fast sprinter so that he can successfully challenge opponents. He should also be able to follow up during corner kicks and try to score.

In my opinion, one of the greatest center fullbacks ever, in modern time, was Giuseppe Bergomi (the now retired Italian footballer). His ability to read the game, play without panic, and have the opponents bounce off him as if he was made of stone, made him feared among any player.

His nickname was Lo zio, which means "uncle" in Italian. This was because of the mustache he wore as a very young player. Bergomi played 20 years at the F.C. Internazionale (F.C Inter) from Milano and made 81 performances in Italy's national team.

Younger players tend to avoid this position as they want to play as high up the field as possible. History shows how the best center backs started their career playing as forwards or offensive midfielders and then moved lower in the field hierarchy.

In my experience, coaches tend to put the most responsible and brave players in the position of fullback because they are supposed to lead the team.

The reason for this is because they need to be responsible for coordinating the rest of the defense line during the opponents attack, and this requires experience and maturity to execute.

You should also know that a team might play with one fullback depending on the formation and the upcoming opponents. Playing with one fullback usually indicates that a team is going to attack more and focus less on defense.

Left & Right Fullback - The Rabbit

The left and right fullbacks are located at their respective sides of the field (see illustration below). The acronyms LB (left fullback) & RB (right fullback) is used to describe these two positions on a tactical dashboard.

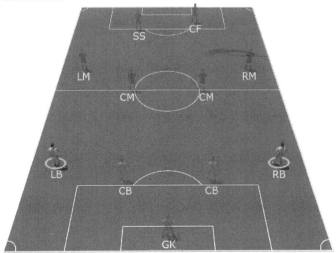

To perform well as left and right fullback, a player has to possess good sprinting abilities, as this position requires a lot of running up and down the field.

Worth mentioning too, is that there is no difference between these two positions when it comes to tactical responsibility. The only real distinction here is that a left fullback is usually left-footed whereas a right fullback is right-footed. This enables them to serve strikers with effective crosses from their respective sides.

One of the greatest left fullback's ever was Paolo Maldini who played for 24 years at the Italian giants, A.C Milan. He possessed great sprinting abilities, plus he was able to serve quality crosses to the strikers.

Furthermore, his marking skills were extraordinary by any standards. When it comes to right fullbacks, I have to mention Brazil's Dani Alves. He is, without any question of doubt, a perfect example of a great modern-day, fullback.

His exceptional skills with the ball, along with his speed and ability to adapt himself both in offense and defense positions, illustrates the requirements beautifully on what it takes to succeed in this position.

Today, a modern left & right fullback is more like a winger with defensive duties. This is without doubts one of the most demanding positions on the soccer field and not many players are able to handle the tactical defensive responsibilities combined with the offensive ones.

Needless to say, without possessing exceptional pace, it is not possible to perform well in the position of either left or right fullback. Bear in mind that opponents challenge fullbacks in dribbling and running duels constantly, which is why this is a really tough position to play well.

Something else worth mentioning is that even if a player is left-footed he might still prefer to play on the right flank. This is often the case when players want to get a better shooting angle. When a left-footed player plays on the right flank, he is able to attack from the flank inside the field rather than just crossing the ball from it.

Wingback - A Blend of Two Positions

The wingback is, as it sounds, a blend of winger and fullback. The placement is either on the left or right of the pitch. The acronyms LWB (left wing back) or RWB (right wing back) is used to describe these positions on a soccer field.

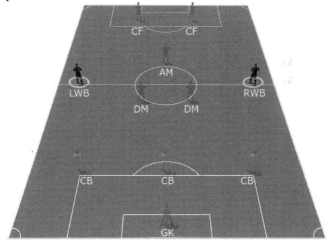

When it comes to performing well as a wingback, the most important skill is to have exceptional stamina (just as with the left & right fullback positions), and also be able to cross the ball with accuracy inside the opponent's 18 yard box.

This is a position where you are expected to have exceptional offensive skills and a big responsibility for defense; a role that can be really hard to pull off. This is why so few players are able to take on this position.

The Brazilian national team often uses wingbacks because of their good use of offensive tactics during the games. However, one of the biggest drawbacks with this position is that wingbacks leave big gaps in defense as a result of these offensive attacks.

One of the most successful wingbacks in modern time is Brazil's Douglas Maicon. He possesses all the necessary skills to master this position, in that he's exceptionally fast, good with the ball, and able to cross it with accuracy inside the 18 yard box.

This is not a position you will see often, at least not in amateur teams, because it requires high levels of stamina. Amateur soccer players tend to focus more on having fun with the ball rather than sprinting up and down 50 yards at a time without even getting to touch it.

Another reason why coaches tend to avoid this position in amateur games is because a player might easily get confused about his true responsibilities because he is playing neither as winger or fullback.

I am telling you this from my own experience. I was once supposed to play as a wingback but because of my inexperience I caused a lot of problems for the team. Consequently, they ended up covering for my mistakes, but hey, that's another story!

Left/Right Midfielder - All About Speed

The left and right midfielders are located at the respective sides of the soccer field (see image). The acronyms LM (left midfielder) and RM (right midfielder) are used to describe this position in the illustration.

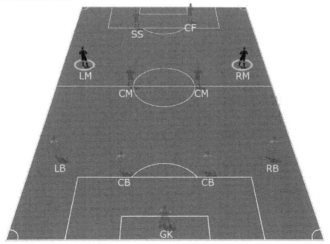

This position can be incredibly boring for a player if the game is located at one side of the field.

For example, if the team is attacking on the right side of the pitch, the left midfielder will seldom get to touch the ball during a game.

In other words, there is a chance a player could spend a lot of time running up and down the field without actually contributing to the game. This not only becomes really tedious, but frustrating too, yet this is a crucial position nonetheless. The key responsibility for defense positions is to cover the respective opponent who plays on the same flank.

The left & right midfielder is one of the most widely used positions in the world of soccer. It is also a part of the 4-4-2 formation which is by far the most popular arrangement among both amateur and professional teams.

The number one requirement a player has to acquire in order to succeed in this position is to be fast, and I mean really, really fast. This is why you will find the fastest soccer players of the team playing as left & right midfielders.

Midfielders must also be able to challenge defenders in dribbling duels, get past them, and lastly, serve well-aimed crosses to the strikers inside the opponent's 18-yard box. Without these abilities, it's impossible play well on the flank.

If I was asked to pick a player that I considered to be the best in this position, then I would pick the Wales speed bullet, Ryan Giggs. His exceptional speed, combined with great ball control, has made him a living nightmare for any defender who crosses him.

He will always be remembered as part of Manchester United's glory days; including the triple they won in the1999 season. It was the time when he was a real nightmare for any defender who confronted him. His ability to dribble past opponents and then serve well-aimed crosses inside the box were unparalleled at that time.

Defensive Midfielder - Inexhaustible Dynamo

The position of defensive midfielder is the one that connects the defense line together with the rest of the team. The acronym DM (defensive midfielder) is used to illustrate this position in the illustration.

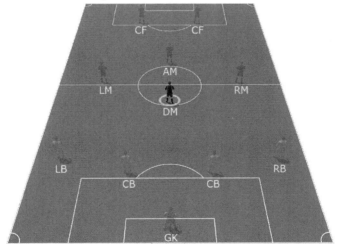

A defensive midfielder is a position - as the name suggests - the closest player to the defense line. His role is to focus on helping the defenders rather than serving strikers with quality passes.

This position might at first sound a little boring, but it actually isn't. The defensive midfielder is responsible for disturbing the ball from defense to the attacking players, meaning his active involvement in the game is high.

Another important part of being defensive midfielder is to encourage teammates when they make mistakes and push them to work harder. In other words, he is someone who aims to boost morale and maintain momentum.

This is also one of the most demanding positions on the field because it requires a lot of hard work both in defense and offense. In short, a defensive midfielder needs to have exceptional stamina and pace in order to play well.

Another necessary skill for playing successful midfielder is the ability to handle the tactical responsibility too, that is, read the game and also constantly work hard without actually receiving a single pass for long periods.

One of the greatest defensive midfielders (if not the best ever) was the outstanding German dynamo, Lothar Matthäus. He combined great tactical and defensive skills with good goal scoring abilities, and also possessed natural leadership qualities.

Lothar Matthäus was one of the main front figures and superstars during the 1994 World Cup in Italy, where he led Germany to victory. He was also voted as the undisputedly best player of the whole tournament.

Central Midfielder - The Nav of The Midfield

This is the position where intelligence meets the ability to make the right tactical decisions on the soccer field. The central midfielder is responsible for holding the ball within the team, moving it from one flank to the other, and serving the strikers with quality passes.

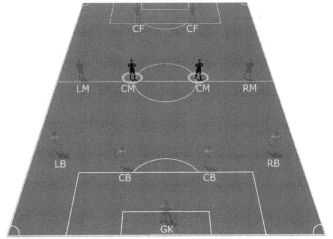

The acronym CM (central midfielder) is used to illustrate this position on the tactical dashboard above. Worth mentioning too, is that a team can also play with just one central midfielder depending on the tactical formation, e.g., 4-3-3.

The central midfielder is also responsible for reading the game, preventing opponents from playing through the central part of the field, and constantly moving the ball from the defense line up to the strikers.

The central midfielder is the player who will generally have more control of the ball than most of others players because of his position. If he fails to complete his task and fall out of the game, the team will suffer greatly in the offensive.

Teams often try to neutralize central midfielders to prevent opponents from utilizing their offensive tactics with any success. This is why a central midfielder needs to be constantly moving as this will make him harder to mark and therefore more difficult to neutralize.

Any team where the central midfielders are not synchronizing with the rest of the players is going to find it really hard to perform well during the game. In other words, if central midfielders fail to perform as expected, then wining is going to become unlikely.

One of the greatest central midfielders ever is the FC Barcelona captain, Xavi Hernandez. His ability to control the ball, dictate the tempo of the game, and his excellent passing skills, are pure art and a sheer pleasure to watch.

Besides winning Champions League several times with "Barcelona" he also led Spain to their first World Cup win in South Africa. If there was a perfect example of a central midfielder, then it would have to be Xavi.

The Winger - Dribbling Wizard

The winger's main mission is to dribble around his defender and find scoring opportunities for himself and the striker. This position is using LW (left winger) and RW (right winger) as illustrated in the image below.

While a winger does not need to equal the strength of a defender, or have the ability to dictate the tempo of a game like a central midfielder, he must, however, be exceptionally fast and able to dribble his opponents.

He should also be able to shoot with accuracy and power. Without these skills, it will be very hard to play as a winger because the focus is on scoring goals.

Failure to score goals as a winger will result in a pretty short career in this position. Many players have tried and failed to become successful wingers, and most will tell you that the pressure is simply inhuman!

If you ask the experts who the best winger ever was, most of them will agree that it was Manuel Francisco dos Santos, known better by his nickname "Garrincha" - the little bird. He led Brazil to two World Cup victories, the first being in Sweden in 1958 and the second in Chile in 1962.

Garrincha was able to dribble past any defender in the world with seeming ease. It appeared to onlookers that there was nothing this skilled winger couldn't do. He possessed great pace combined with an incredibly accurate shooting ability. He was also famous for something else, something related to a physical condition.

Because his left leg was a whole 2.4 inches shorter than the right one, he was accused of having an unfair advantage. Some players claimed that this disparity gave him an undeserved benefit on the soccer field, saying that it was responsible for his exceptional control of the ball.

Today, the undisputedly best winger in the world has to be the Argentinean Lionel Messi. His exceptional speed with the ball, along with his dribbling and shooting skills, are out of this world and a privilege to witness.

Beside all these superlatives and exceptional skills used to describe the raw talent of Messi, he is also considered to be the most complete soccer player of all time. This is because of his ability to master an entire range of soccer skills and successfully incorporate them into his games.

Striker - Mission, Scoring Goals

I am sure you already know this, but I will mention it anyway, and that is the striker's job is to score goals, pure and simple. Any striker who stops scoring goals is a striker no more, which is why this position is the most demanding one in the game of soccer.

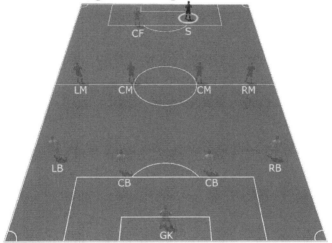

The position of striker is referred to as S (striker) in the illustration above. Note how he is also the closest player in the team to the opponent's goal. This is pretty obvious considering his job is to score.

When playing the position of striker, one has to be prepared for pain and sacrifice. The defenders will do anything and everything within their power to prevent him from scoring. It goes without saying, therefore, that strikers often get a lot of bashings because of their position.

I am sure you have watched a soccer game, either LIVE or on TV, and often noticed a striker jogging around and perhaps even looking uninterested when it comes to defending or taking that extra run for the team.

Such behavior is actually the true nature of a striker. Remember, his job is to score goals, not chase opponents. A striker knows he just needs one chance to score, so he conserves all his energy for that right moment.

For anyone not fully attuned to the game of soccer, seeing a striker waiting idly by can be annoying and irritating to watch. It's important to know, however, that this has nothing to do with disrespect for the game or the team, and everything to do with the tactical play of a striker.

Choosing the best player for a specific position can be a really tough and difficult decision at times, and one that can often be controversial.

But get it right by selecting the right man for the right job and it's like awarding the team with a license to win. In my opinion, the best striker ever picked (at least in modern time), is Brazil's Ronaldo Luís Nazário de Lima.

He was simply amazing. He gave credit to all the clubs he ever played for, but was probably at his best during the World Cup of 2002 in Japan/South Korea. Ronaldo scored most goals in the tournament (two in the final) and led Brazil to their fifth World Cup victory.

His amazing high speed dribbling skills, and ability to score goals with both feet, made him a frightening challenge for defenders from all over the world.

Goalkeeper - The Last Outpost

Playing as a goalkeeper is without doubt the most important position of the whole team. Describing the responsibility a goalie carries on his shoulders is really hard to do. In order to understand this fully you must experience it firsthand!

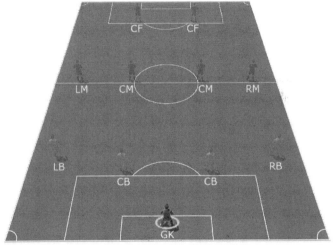

A goalkeeper is marked as GK (goalkeeper) in the illustration above, and is the last outpost in the team.

While the job of goalkeeper might seem lucrative and fun, it can also be pretty boring in situations where one team dominates the game.

In such cases, the keeper will barely touch the ball, if ever, and the minutes can feel like hours to him.

On the losing side, a goalkeeper can become overwhelmed by the sheer number of shots that come his way, especially if the opponents manage to score, and particularly if they manage to score more than once.

As well as preventing the opponents from scoring through sacrificing himself for the team by diving head first into situations where a player just might have his foot, a goalkeeper is also supposed to organize his defense line.

Another part of the game where a goalie plays a crucial role is to continuously encourage his teammates no matter what mistakes they might have made on the field. As you can see, a goalkeeper is also an incredibly important position to hold in the game of soccer.

Whenever anyone asks who the best ever goalkeeper was in the game of soccer, there's a good chance you will hear this name: Lev Yashin, nicknamed, "The Black Spider" or "The Black Panther." He was from the former USSR and had amazing reflexes. He was indeed an extraordinary athlete and perhaps the best goalkeeper ever known in the history of the game.

Yashin played for Dynamo Moscow, and also saved over 150 penalties during his active career! This is a really impressive fact when you consider that many outfield players never score half that number of goals during their entire soccer career.

To summarize then; goalkeeping is the position where no mistakes are allowed. Even a tiny slipup might result in the team losing a match.

Also, a goalkeeper who is not totally confident in his ability is going to subconsciously convey this message to the rest of the team, something which will indirectly decrease the performance of the other players.

Second Striker - The Deep Lying Forward

The position of the second striker is usually a few yards behind the center forward. The acronyms SS (second striker) is used to illustrate this position in the illustration below.

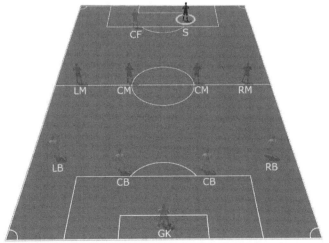

The main aim of a second striker is as the name suggests: to score as many goals as possible.

However, because of his position, he is also the player who is supposed to create scoring opportunities for the central forward as well.

While a second striker doesn't have to be equally as quick as a central forward, he should still be able to perform fast, controlled runs into free space. Another important difference is that a second striker must pose an exceptional understanding for the game.

Often, he will be the one who serves the central forward with scoring opportunities, and therefore must be smart enough to find a way through the opponent's well-oiled defense. Without these traits, it's impossible to succeed in this position.

Everyone has their favorite soccer greats, and even the undisputed players will be disputed by some. However, if I was asked to pick the best second striker of all time, I would choose the former Netherlands footballer, Dennis Bergkamp. Besides being an incredible asset in the national team, he was also considered to be one of the legends of London's pride, Arsenal FC.

His extraordinary understanding of the game and his ability to create scoring opportunities and score goals from nothing and nowhere, made him feared among all defenders of that time.

You just never knew what he was about to do next, and during his very best moments he was perhaps even the best player on the planet.

Centre Forward - The Speed Bullet

This is the position for those types of players who are exceptionally fast. These guys are able to make quick decisions and are skilled at creating great finishing opportunities. Without these traits, it is literally impossible to succeed in this position.

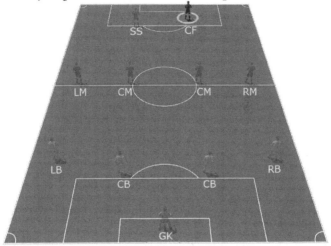

The acronym CF (central forward) is used to show this position on the illustration above. The main job of a central forward is to score, but unlike a striker, he should be able to run into free space. The striker, on the other hand, is best described as a target player.

The "target" refers to his ability to receive the ball and keep it out of reach of the opponents while the rest of the team moves higher up the field into position.

Beside the traits mentioned in the beginning of this chapter, playing as central forward is a position where the player has to be prepared for a degree of unfair or rough treatment from the opponents.

They will do everything within their ability to stop him from finding and creating goal scoring opportunities.

This might involve anything from delivering small punches, tugging on a shirt when the referee's back is turned in an attempt to pull the centre forward off balance, or by verbal tormenting, either mocking performance or attacking the player's personality.

All this might sound a bit scary and unacceptable, but like it or not, this is often how it is out there on the field.

Such behavior goes on because defenders know that if they give just one gentlemanly opportunity, then the chances of a centre forward scoring increase dramatically.

So, who do I consider to be the best centre forward in the modern times? Well, the answer might surprise you if you have followed soccer in the past, but I would definitely pick West Germany's former player Jurgen Klinsmann.

The reason why I consider him to be the best of the best is because of his ability to run into free space, control the ball at high speed, and most important of all, his talent to follow through at the end.

He was also part of the best German team ever who won the 1990 World Cup that was held in Italy. Here, Germany literally crushed all opponents with their fast-paced and highly-efficient attacking approach.

Attacking Midfielder - The Mastermind

This is the position where the player needs to be a master at reading the game and have a natural ability to solve difficult situations. He must also be able to surprise the opponents. The acronym AM (attacking midfielder) is used to show the position on the illustration below.

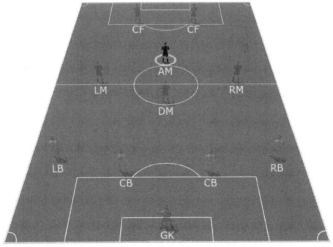

Other critical skills required to succeed in this position are physical and mental stamina, the confidence to challenge opponents one-on-one, and maintain total poise at all times.

Whenever a team is being selected, picking the best player for a specific position is never an easy task, especially when there's a good pool or talent to choose from.

It's not unusual to hear a lot of disagreement when various positions are allocated to certain players. However, when it comes to the attacking midfielder, most players will agree with the choice because this is not a position that all players can, or want to undertake.

The player I would personally nominate as the best attacking midfielder of all time, as I write, is the retired Argentine footballer, Diego Armando Maradona.

Although the soccer superstar of the 1980s, he is still considered - even today - to be the best footballer the world has ever known among his adoring fans around the globe.

Maradona mastered all necessary skills to succeed in this position. His creativity was really something unique to him, and if you haven't seen him play, then I would suggest you look him up on YouTube, because this guy is simply amazing to watch during the height of his soccer career in the late eighties.

He led Argentina to a victory in the Mexico World Cup and also scored the goal that was voted as the best goal ever to be scored against England.

This was when he dribbled six of their players, and then finished off by putting the ball gently into the net masks. I doubt anyone will ever score such a goal during a World Cup competition again.

Learning the Main Soccer Rules

I know by experience that understanding all the soccer rules can be confusing at times and cause a lot of headaches.

When I first started to play soccer I had enormous problems with several of these rules. This is why I am going to look at them in more detail in this section, so that you don't have to struggle as much as I did back then.

For example, I would run into offside numerous times before I figured out why my teammates were shouting "Mirsad, you are standing offside, MOVE!"

The funny thing was, back then I didn't have a clue where to move to, so I just kept running until they stopped shouting.

However, once I grasped the basics and realized that it was actually easier than I had thought, a whole new world opened up to me. Suddenly I could enjoy watching and playing soccer without needing to ask about every little decision the referee made.

Another important aspect you should be aware of is that of the human factor. This is something that can greatly affect the outcome of a soccer rule that has been breached.

What I mean by that is one referee might impose a rule correctly, whereas another might turn a blind eye, even though it's clear that an infringement has occurred.

One of the best examples of this is the goal Diego Armando Maradona scored during the 1986 World Cup. Here he used his hand to punch the ball over England's then goalkeeper, Peter Shilton, just as he was about to grip the ball.

Although the whole world witnessed Maradona using his hand to score that goal, the referee counted it as a legit goal and gave Argentina an early 1-0 lead over England. Maradona scored the best goal ever in the same game, but that's another story.

My point is that rules must always be followed, but there will always be a human factor that decides whether they will be spotted or acted upon, or not. Although one referee might give a red card in a specific situation, another might not even warrant a same or similar violation with a foul.

This is something you need to bear in mind, whether your aim is to start playing soccer or just understanding the fundamentals of the game so that you can enjoy watching it with more knowledge.

Now, let's start to look at the rules in more detail. The first one we will go over is the field of play and its markings.

Field of Play and its Markings

The field of play consists either of artificial or natural grass. In any case, the field must remain green which means that other colors are not allowed in soccer.

Of course, other circumstances like weather could make a pitch look more like brown muddy farming land than a soccer field, but the point is its natural color is green, and how it ends up after a game, or a storm, is just one of those things that can't be controlled in an outdoor environment.

Whenever a soccer field has been altered by the weather prior to a game, a referee is allowed to inspect the ground and make a decision about whether the field is playable or not. A regular soccer pitch is rectangular in shape and consists of different lines that are clearly marked in white, and these must be visible to the players.

In the illustrations below you will find the markings of a soccer pitch. They should be self-explanatory so I won't bore you by going over what they represent in micro detail.

End Line (Goal Line)

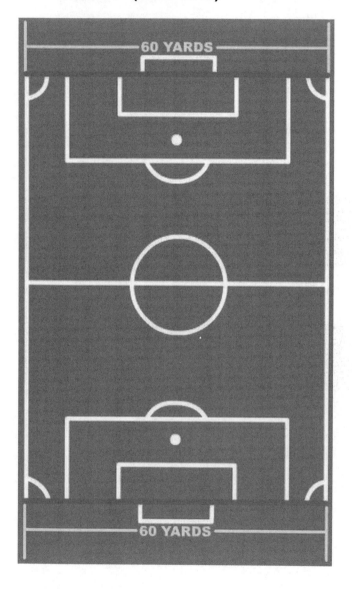

Sideline (Touch Line)

Goal

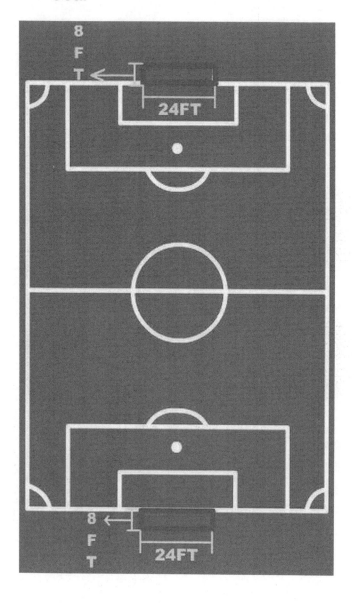

Goal Box

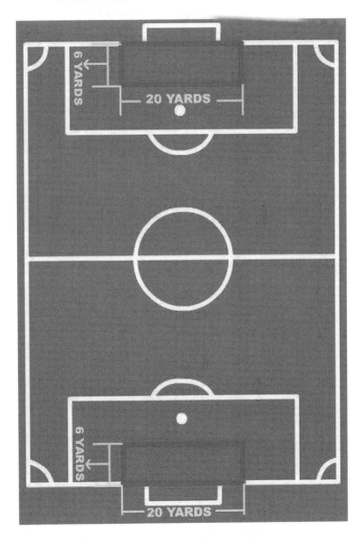

Penalty Box

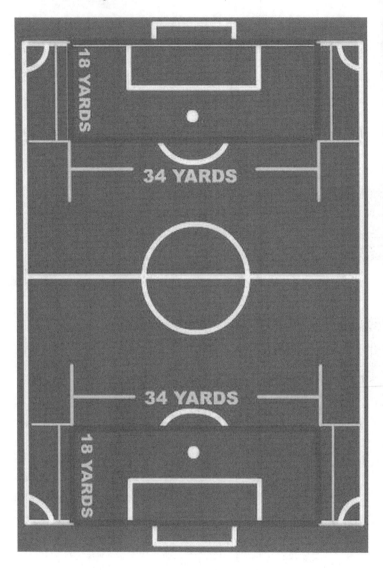

Center Circle

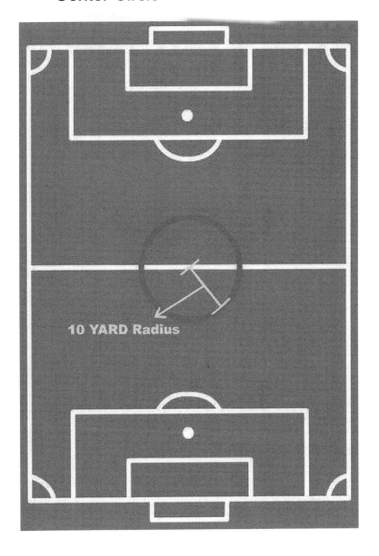

10 YARD Radius

Halfway Line

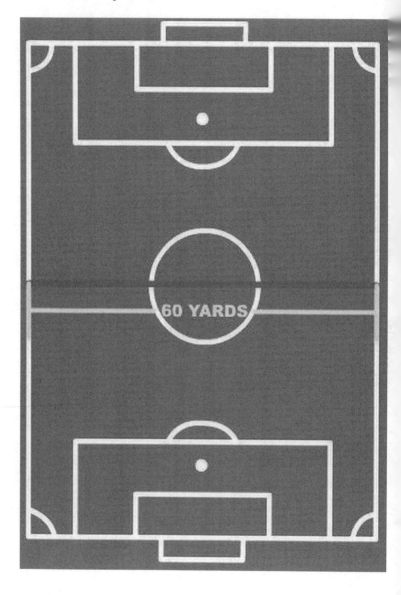

Penalty Box Arc

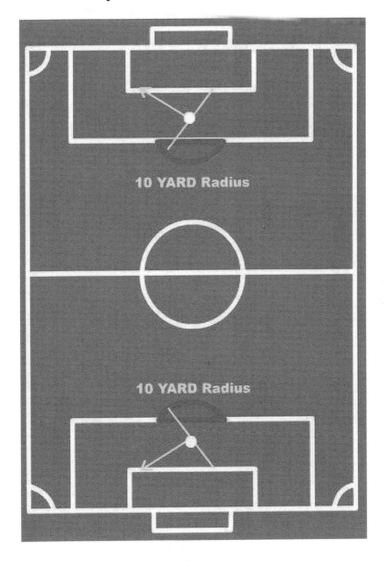

Corner Arc

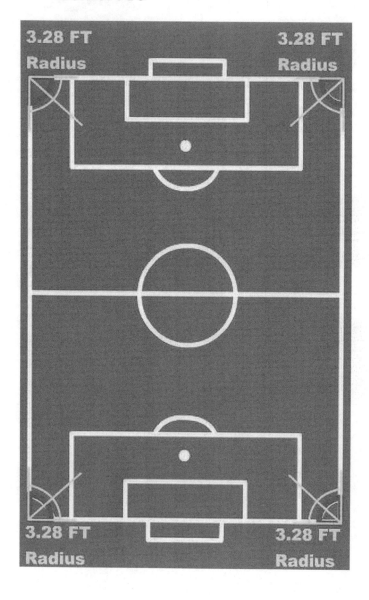

Number of Players on the Field

A regular game is played by two teams typically separated into different jersey colors, e.g., blue and red.

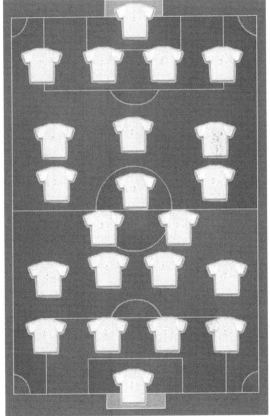

Each team cannot consist of more than 11 players and one of these must act as the goalkeeper wearing a jersey of different color. The referee will not allow the game to start if a team has less than 7 players on the field.

FIFA, Confederation & National Competitions

In regular competitions regulated by FIFA, a team can only use three substitutes per game. No exceptions or agreements to this rule can be made with the referee.

Non-Competition Games

Non-competitive games often include friendly and pre-season matches where the focus is not so much on winning, but allowing as many players as possible to get time, and therefore experience, on the field. In these games, a maximum of five substitutes is allowed if both teams have reached an agreement beforehand.

Player Registration

Before the start of a game, there must be list of all the players participating. This list typically includes the player's full names and birthdates. This register is mandatory and a game cannot start without having the referee inspecting and approving it prior to the match.

The Players Equipment (Kit)

In this chapter I will go through the typical kit that a player wears during both practice sessions and actual games. I will also explain the common rules attached to each item.

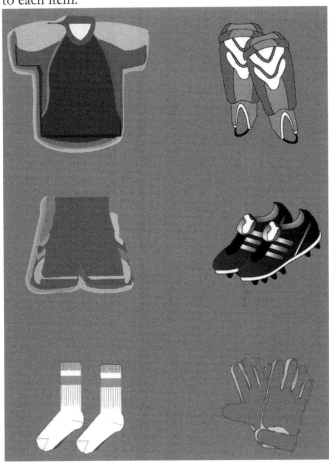

Shin Guards

As a soccer player, you must wear your shin guards during both practice and competition. Your shin guards are also required to be approved by your soccer association.

Besides offering shin protection, wearing shin guards is essential for insurance purposes too. They will ensure any costs are covered should you be unlucky enough to injure your legs during a game or practice session.

The Jersey

Your jersey must match the colors of the rest of your teammates, excluding the goalkeeper, who must wear a jersey distinguishable from the rest of the team.

A funny trend has become popular in recent years where players use math to create the number they want to wear. For example, several professional players have used 1+8 which is 9 because the number was already taken by another player.

Shorts

Just as with the jersey, the color of the shorts must match the rest of the team, excluding the goalkeeper. You are allowed to wear thermal undershorts but they should have the same color as your visible shorts.

Stockings

Even your stockings must match those of the rest of the team. They should also cover the whole shin guard, although some players prefer to have the shin guards stick out a bit for some reason, and will do this unless they get a verbal warning by the referee.

Cleats

When it comes to cleats (studs on the sole of the shoe) you are actually allowed to wear different ones. I've done this several times simply by taking a cleat from one pair and combining it with the cleat of another pair.

This will not help you play better but the "cool" factor is high, and you will definitely stand out from the other players on the field.

Gloves

The gloves of a keeper should distinguish him from the players and referees. An outfield player is not allowed to run around wearing keeper's gloves if he is not playing as goalie.

Fouls & Misconduct

There are many different fouls & misconducts in the game of soccer. In this chapter we will look at the most common ones, how they occur, and when they are issued.

Direct Free Kick

A direct free kick occurs when an opponent commits a foul on the other player by playing irresponsibly.

This usually occurs by missing a sliding tackle, using arms in heading duels, and by pushing and shoving an opponent to gain control of the ball. How often a team is awarded with the free kick depends on the referee and his individual judgment.

Even when a team and their supporters believe a free kick should definitely be given, the referee may still not agree, and at the end of the day, it is his decision that counts.

Indirect Free Kick

An indirect free kick is a method of restarting play in a game of soccer. Unlike the "direct free kick," a goal cannot not be scored straight from the kick, meaning a player must touch the ball first before attempting a goal. In other words, there must be a pass before a player can shoot.

Yellow Card Offences

The yellow card simply means that a player has committed an offence that is not acceptable on the soccer field.

This can be a specific type of behavior like throwing the ball at the coach of the opposing team, using inappropriate language, or by committing a foul that a referee considers deliberate and therefore worth issuing a yellow card for.

As always, there will often be one referee who considers something a yellow card offence, whereas another one might not. In short, this means two identical situations could have a very different outcome depending on the ref.

Red Card Offences

The red card is issued after the second yellow card, but a player might receive it directly as well if the circumstances warrant it.

Typical situations where a red card is given are when a player unfairly tackles an opponent, argues or insults the referee using inappropriate language, or by interrupting a goal scoring opportunity using the arms.

Again, while one referee might consider an incident being a red card offence, another might not even give the player a yellow card in the same or similar situation.

Procedure of Penalty Kick

The penalty kick occurs when a player performs an offence against an opponent. Some of the most common reasons for this are a missed challenge (where the player tackles the opponent instead of the ball), playing rough, and pushing or pulling the jersey of an opponent.

For a penalty kick to be awarded for the offence it must occur inside the 18 yard box (see field of play).

Before taking a penalty kick the ball must be placed on the penalty mark. It will not be allowed to go ahead if the one taking the penalty tries to move the ball closer or further from the goal in an attempt to get a better position.

Sometimes, the white point will be completely devastated and it can be hard to kick the ball properly from it.

If this is the case, the referee must be made aware of it. The player needs to let him know that he can't perform a proper penalty kick under these circumstances.

I've done it several times myself during my soccer career and providing the complaint is justified, a referee will usually allow the ball to be moved no more than a ¼ yard to where the ground is greener and less disturbed.

The one taking the penalty kick is allowed to move outside the 18 yard box in order to generate more speed and power for the kick. However, the other players are not allowed to run inside the 18 yard box until the ball has been kicked. If they do, the penalty must be retaken.

One caution I want to raise here is that all rules described in this chapter are not applicable during a penalty kick shootout. In these situations, the player has one chance to score and he can't take any rebounds if say the ball bounces off a goal post or cross bar.

Naturally, goalkeepers love shootouts because they have absolutely nothing to lose. The players, on the other hand, are forced to score if, and if they fail to do so, they may just become the scapegoat for the losing side and experience the pain and misery from their missed penalty.

You should also know that the player who was fouled inside the 18 yard box is not supposed to take the penalty.

Usually, the team has already decided before the game who will take any penalties should they occur, and also his substitute, if say the main choice gets injured or sent off for whatever reason during the match.

So these are the main things you need to know about penalty. Unless your ambition is to become an international referee, then the details about penalty kicks in this chapter should be more than enough.

The Role of Assistant Referee's

Assistant referees are the guys you see running up and down the sidelines during a game. Their role is to monitor the game just like a regular referee.

They also wear the same clothes as the main referee. The key difference between assistant referees and the main ref is that they have a flag they use to draw attention to any breach of the rules.

The main duty of an assistant referee is to decide when players run into offside, but they can also make the main referee aware of other situations that he might have missed.

A common situation might be when a player touches the ball with his hand inside the 18 yard box and the main referee misses it.

In most case, if the assistant referee lets him know about this he will award the opposing team with a penalty kick.

Just as an assistant referee can point out a penalty kick to the main ref, he can also make him aware of any unfair play that he sees.

Depending on the situation, this can sometimes result in a red card. In short, assistant referees are the main ref's extra set of eyes.

In all FIFA regulated international games there must also be a fourth referee. He is responsible for handling the substitutes of both teams and usually wears a different color shirt.

The fourth ref is easily recognizable because he stands in the area located in the middle of the substitute benches.

This referee is also responsible for presenting the stoppage time accumulated during a game. He does this by lifting a digital board which displays the added time.

The stoppage time is typically collected during the different game breaks, such as taking care of injured players, or the time taken to bring on substitutes.

However, it is the main referee who finally gets to decide how much time is going to be added. The fourth referee is also responsible for monitoring the behavior of the players on the bench.

If he encounters a player, or even a coach, behaving inappropriately, especially by bellowing offensive language, then he can make the main referee aware of this. Such behavior can result in a yellow or red card being issued.

I know what you are probably thinking: how can a coach or a player on the bench get a yellow or red card considering that they are not even playing?

Well, put simply, the same rules that apply to the outfield players also apply to the coach and the substitutes as they are still part of the overall game.

To Be or Not to Be Offside

In my experience, the offside is the most confusing rule in soccer. Personally, I had enormous problems understanding it when I first began my soccer career.

I remember how my teammates would shout "OFFSIDE" as soon as I entered the opponents half of the field at an inappropriate time.

I just could not understand it until I eventually sat down and carefully read, and reread a chapter on the rule. Although there was a lot of jargon, and some confusing examples to grasp, I did finally get it after a few days.

In fact, once I fully understood the offside rule it was actually quite simple to comprehend. It seems, therefore, that I was making a major issue out of something that was actually pretty simple to follow.

The two illustrations below are simplified versions of what I learned from the book. They should also help you to understand the rule easier and without getting bogged down with microanalysis as I did.

Player Offside

In the first illustration the player with the ball is offside because he was already past the opponent's last player when the ball was passed to him.

So a player is in an offside position when he is closer to the opponent's goal line than the ball and the second-to-last defender. I might still sound a bit confusing until you've read and discussed it a few times, but try not to think too much.

Most strikers like to lure a half yard behind the defense line. Then, the moment the ball is passed, they simply wait a brief moment before making a dash for the ball.

By waiting a second, the striker is able to avoid being offside. This is because he received the ball while the last player was behind him. This means he is still onside because the ball was passed when he was onside.

Player Onside

The other side of the rule is being onside which is equally controversial as being offside.

In the illustration the ball is passed to the player while he has the last player in front of him which means that he is onside.

You should also know also that each referee has a different view on what he considers to be offside and onside, depending where he is when the rule is supposedly broken.

It comes down to the human factor again, which means the ref may simply miss the offence; something that can result in a catastrophe for the affected team.

There may also be a case where a side referee reports the breach, but the main referee disagrees with him and allows the game to continue despite the raised flag going up (see offside rule illustration).

The best way to learn this rule is to watch a LIVE game and study the referee's decisions. In most cases you will notice that you and the referee do not agree on what's offside or not.

This just means that you have a different view on a given situation, and differences of opinion are all part of soccer.

Duration of The Game

A regular adult soccer game lasts for two halves with each half being 45 minutes long. These halves can actually be less than 40 minutes but both teams need to agree on this pre-game, and also notify the referee – obviously!

In youth soccer, each half is usually played for 30 minutes, Furthermore, any substitutions are often made on the fly, which means that there is little, or no stoppage time added to the match.

The main reason why rules are more laid back with youth soccer is the fact that kids are supposed to have fun on the field and not get sidetracked by adults' rules.

Once a player turns 11 years old though, he is expected to start paying attention to stoppage time and develop an understanding on how it affects the outcome of a game.

The half time break in soccer is 15 minutes maximum. During this break, players are rehydrating, focusing on correcting any mistakes made during the first half, and listening to the coaches' tactical instructions.

When break time is up, the referee usually blows his whistle in front of each team's locker room or just bangs on the door to make them aware that it's time to resume play.

If you have been going through this book from the very beginning you will have read about the stoppage time in the "assistant referee's" chapter. Without running the risk of sounding like a parrot, I will just mention the situations that are common for adding stoppage time:

- Each time a substitution is performed.
- Taking care of injured players.
- Special breaks (e.g. hydration).

During playoff games, there is something called extra time. It consists of two halves with each being 15 minutes in duration. It works in the same way as regular play time (45 minutes) where the teams must switch the sides after each half.

If there are no goals scored during this time, then a penalty shootout is bought in to determine the winning team. A penalty shootout is not regulated by any specific time frame, although players can't procrastinate and waste time.

This is about all you need to know about the duration of soccer games.

Restarting the Game with a Goal Kick

A goal kick is used to restart the game after an opponent has kicked the ball over the goal line during an attack on the opposing team. In other words, if the red team is attacking the goal of the blue team and kicks the ball past the goal line, a goal kick is given to the blue team.

No players are allowed inside the 18-yard box when the goal kick is performed. If a player on the same team as the goalkeeper receives the ball inside the 18 yard box, then the referee will get the goalkeeper to re-take the goal kick.

However, a team player can actually perform the goal kick if a goalie is not skillful enough to kick the ball far or if he has a specific injury that prevents him from kicking the ball with any real force.

I did this quite a bit during my soccer career because we had a goal keeper who couldn't kick the ball further than 10 yards.

Before taking a goal kick, the ball should be completely still and placed on the long side of the goal box. Another thing worth mentioning is that the ball can actually be placed anywhere along the horizontal edge of the goal box.

As an opponent, you are allowed to jump in the path of the ball as long as it is out of the 18 yard box, but you are not allowed to shout or do anything to disrupt a goal kick before or while it is being taken.

I've seen players get sent off the field because of disrupting behavior during a goal kick. For some reason, referees tend to be less tolerant of bad behavior towards a goalkeeper than they are to other players on the soccer field.

One interesting fact that you should know about the goal kick is that you can score directly from it if you are able to kick the ball right over to the other side of the field. Mind you, this is a really hard thing to do as it requires a huge amount of power and accuracy.

As you can see, the goal kick rule is pretty easy to understand and doesn't require a lot of thought in order to be understood. Just think of it as a method used to restart the game whenever necessary.

Committing a Penalty Kick

I first came across the rule of a penalty kick during my first ever game. Before the match, the coach had me warm up, and after 15 minutes of sweating and doing all kind of exercises, I was ready to jump into the game.

I can remember how the coach took me to one side before the game started and said: "Mirsad, listen. Whatever you do, please don't try to tackle a player inside the 18 yard box."

I looked at him and said, don't worry coach I won't. Then, as soon as I entered the field, I hadn't been playing more than five minutes before I tackled an opponent inside the 18 yard box!

OK, so let me now explain this (sometimes confusing) rule. A penalty kick is given when a player commits a foul on a rival player inside the 18 yard box (see field of play).

When this happens (and depending on the severity of the foul), the referee might award the other team with a penalty. A penalty kick can also be awarded to the rival side if a player commits handball inside his own 18 yard box.

In general, any offence committed inside the 18 yard can result in a penalty kick, but not always. Although a given situation might look as though it deserves a penalty kick, the end decision rests with the referee.

Sometimes, he might not agree and allow the game to continue on despite any protests from the players and their spectators.

This is why you will sometimes see players giving the referee hassle after he refuses to blow his whistle on what they consider to be a violation by the opposing side.

Such displays of discontent usually fall onto deaf ears though as the rule of soccer says that a referee always has the final word.

During a penalty kick, only the player taking it and the goalkeeper are allowed to be inside the 18 yard box. If any other players enter it before the ball is kicked, then the penalty has to be re-taken.

However, all players are allowed to sprint into the 18 yard box the moment the ball is kicked. The same players are also allowed to score from eventual rebounds that might occur from the kick.

One more thing you should know is that the goal keeper is allowed to run along the side line but he is not permitted to move toward the ball.

Sometimes he might take a chance and try gaining half a yard by doing this, but if he's spotted, the referee will more than likely order the penalty kick to be retaken.

Direct & Indirect Free Kick

In soccer, there are two types of free kicks, namely indirect and direct. The "direct" free kick occurs much more often than an "indirect" one.

The main difference between these two is that a direct free kick can be aimed directly at the goal whereas an indirect free kick must be touched first by a teammate before a shot can be taken at the goal.

Progression of a Direct Free Kick

The direct free kick is taken outside the penalty area (the 18 yard box). As I already mentioned, it can be kicked directly at the goal.

During the kick there will always be a wall of players standing in the path of the ball in an attempt to obstruct it (see illustration above).

This line up of players is there to help the goalkeeper cover one side of the goal.

These players must stand 10 yards from the ball (although many teams tend to move forward a yard in order to make it more difficult for the opponent to kick the ball over the wall and into the goal).

Progression of Indirect Free Kick

As pointed out in the beginning of this chapter, an indirect free kick means the ball must at least be touched by a second player before a shot can be taken at the goal.

Another difference is that an indirect free kick can occur inside the penalty box.

Just as with the direct free kick, there is also a wall of players to help the keeper cover the goal.

This wall of players must be 10 yards from the ball until it is in play. The ball is "in play" the moment it is struck.

The Art of Corner Kick

The corner kick is a method used to restart the game. It is given when a player of the defending teams kicks the ball over the goal line. In the illustration below, the corner kick is awarded to the red team.

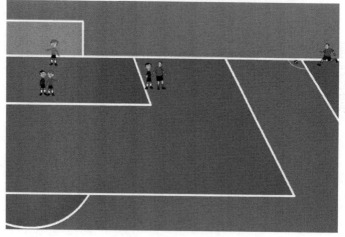

Another common situation where a corner kick is given is when a player from say the red team kicks the ball and it touches one of the blue players, and then passes the goal line without making any contact with a player from the red team.

A corner kick is taken from the right if the ball passes on the left side of the goal and vice versa.

The ball must remain inside the corner arc, though it can be moved within it. Players from the rival team are not allowed to be any closer than 10 yards to one taking the corner kick.

The player taking the corner kick can kick the ball inside the 18 yard box and hope that one of his teammates gets a chance to score from there.

However, if the one taking the corner kick is skilled, he can also try to curve the ball directly into the goal from the corner.

This is something that is one of the most difficult things to do in soccer, but there are some players who are able to pull it off.

Also worth mentioning is that the player taking the kick is only allowed to strike the ball once (just as with the direct free kick).

The only time he can contact it a second time is when an opponent or a teammate touches the ball after he has kicked it.

Throw-in Jargon

It took me a while to figure out why the referee was blowing in his whistle each time I performed a throw-in and then gave it to the other team. The throw-in is given once the ball passes the side lines of either side.

In the illustration below, a player from the red team touched the ball last before it went over the side line.

That means the blue team is awarded the throw-in (similar principle to the corner kick)

When performing a throw-in, a player must keep his feet on the ground and stand completely behind the side line. He must also make sure he pulls the ball right behind his head before throwing it into the pitch.

If the player doing the throw-in happens to lose grip and drop the ball, then the other team is awarded the throw-in instead. Dropping the ball is something that can happen when the weather is wet and the ball is slippery.

Rival players are not allowed to disturb the one who is about to perform the throw-in. For example, an opponent is not allowed to jump around in front of him, shout things out, and certainly not allowed to use any kind of offensive language or gestures as a method to put him off.

Opponents are also required to stand at least two yards away from the player performing the throw-in. If any of these rules are not adhered to and respected, the referee can, and often does, issue the opponent with a yellow card.

If a player already has one yellow card, he can still get a second one, or face a red card, and also get sent off the field at the referee's discretion.

Ball in and Out of Play

Ball in Play

As a spectator it can often be difficult to figure out when the ball is in play or not. To keep things simple, a ball is considered to be in play as long as it doesn't pass either the goal or side lines.

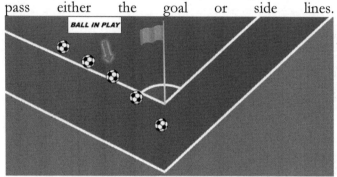

BALL IN PLAY

If a player kicks the ball and it hits the posts of the goal, a corner post, or even the assistant referee, and then bounces back onto the field, then it is still considered to be in play.

Ball out of Play

There is an important aspect of this rule that's worth noting though. Whenever a part of the ball passes the line, it does not mean it's out of play.

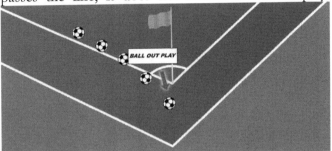

The FIFA rules state that a ball must be completely over the line for it to be out of play (see image above).

Size, Weight and Pressure of the Ball

There are different types of soccer balls which are used depending on the level of competition being played.

Generally speaking, the higher the competition the more requirements are put on the quality of the ball. Some of the general guidelines are as follows:

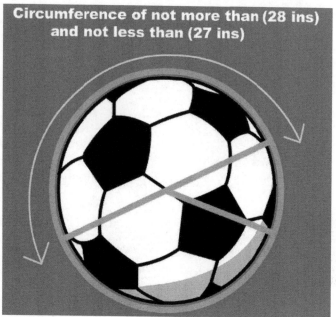

Circumference of not more than (28 ins) and not less than (27 ins)

- The ball's circumference should be no bigger than 28" and not be less than 27".
- The weight should not exceed 16 oz. and has to be a minimum weight of 14oz.
- The pressure of the ball should be somewhere between 8.5– 15.6 lbs/sq.

Soccer balls used in adult competition must be issued by FIFA and also sport the international match ball logo.

There are generally several copies of the same ball available at the sides of the field and also one behind each goal.

If a ball goes out of play, for whatever reason, it can be quickly replaced by the back-up balls, thus allowing the game to continue with a minimum of disruption.

Although it doesn't occur very often, there are occasions when a ball bursts. In most cases this is because it's over pumped with air which obviously results in too much pressure. Obviously in the case of a burst soccer ball, the game is stopped until it's replaced.

Whenever a game has to be restarted like this, the referee drops the new ball between two players from opposing teams. The one who gets the first touch on the ball is usually the one who gains possession of it, unless of course it bounces over to another player.

Back in time, soccer balls were made of leather and pretty simple in their construction. Today however, the manufacturing of soccer balls has exploded into a huge industry where companies pump millions of dollars into the precision development of their products.

The manufacturing of modern soccer balls has become something of a science.

Barely a year goes by without some company claiming to have developed the most extraordinary ball of all time, guaranteeing that "their ball" will contribute to a player's technique, enhance powerful shooting, and improve overall accuracy. Personally, I think this is all hogwash!

Method of Scoring

In order to score in soccer, the ball must completely pass the goal line. If it just happens to brush past the goal entrance, the referee will allow the game to continue.

Back in early days of soccer, there were occasions where referees had a tough time knowing for sure whether the whole ball, or just part of the ball, had actually passed the goal line or not.

Today however, making the decision of whether a ball completely goes over the goal line or not is a lot less controversial. During the World Cup in South Africa (2010), FIFA introduced a fifth referee to the game.

His role is to observe behind the goals of respective teams, and one of his main tasks is to monitor the ball as it's played around the goal area.

One interesting situation is a goal that was scored by England in the World Cup final against West Germany. The result was 2-2 and the match was into extra time. One of the England players fired a shot that went under the cross bar and then bounced on the goal line.

The Germans claimed the ball was not over the goal line completely, although the referee thought otherwise and gave England a 3-2 lead in the final. The game ended at 4-2 to England, but still to this day people debate whether that ball was in or out.

So controversial was that goal, an expert from the Department of Engineering Science at the University of Oxford got involved.

His research concluded that the ball was not completely over the goal line which has now raised the debate about who were the true champions of the World Cup in 1966.

A player can use all parts of his body - apart from the hands or arms - to score goals. You may have seen the odd occasion where a player scored with his arm, but such goals are only allowed if a referee misses them, and not because they are valid goals.

The same rules for scoring apply to goalkeepers too. In fact, a goalkeeper can score in the exact same way as a field player, meaning he can head the ball, take free kicks, penalties, and so on.

In most cases, a goalkeeper will usually sprint up the 18-yard box while one of his teammates prepares to cross the ball from a corner kick. This is a desperate attempt to equalize and although the chances of scoring are not high, a keeper can still cause upset inside the box.

To summarize this chapter: In order to score a goal the whole ball must cross the goal line. Remember too, that neither the arms nor the hands can be used for scoring, but all other parts of the body can be utilized for getting that ball into the net.

Starting and Restarting a Game (The Kick-off)

If the rules of soccer are still relatively new to you, then you probably wonder how a game is actually started and restarted.

The beginning of a game is pretty straight forward. There is actually very little preamble prior to the kickoff. It begins by the players taking to the field and then the lead referee and captains of both sides all shake hands.

One other benefit of winning the coin duel is the opportunity to choose which goal to attack in the first half of the match.

The winning team might decide to switch sides because of the poor quality of the field, or because the sun will be in their goalkeeper's eyes.

The teams must also switch sides before the start of the second half. The kickoff I mentioned before is also used to restart the game after a goal is scored.

On rare occasions, you might get to experience a goal that is scored as a direct result of a kickoff. However, scoring directly from a kickoff is unusual because of the distance involved.

This distance gives the goalkeeper plenty of time to position himself in preparation to stop the shot.

In international games there is a bit more pageantry at the start of a match. Here, both teams switch pennants of their respective sides and country as a way to show their respect and appreciation towards the opponents.

This spectacle is done during a major competition (e.g. world cup) or a friendly game (e.g. between two clubs from different countries).

The switch of the pennants and coin duel is carried out by the respective captains of each team. The captains are identifiable by the captain's armband.

Fundamental Soccer

In this section I will explain and illustrate some of the most frequently used ways to play soccer.

This chapter will help you get a fundamental understanding of how the game of soccer is actually played.

I want you to know that there are countless combinations on how these skills can be combined and adapted to suite the style of an individual player.

This means they can be utilized from different positions, players distance, parts of the field, and so on.

The common denominator for all of these skills is that they are used at all levels of the game. In other words, from the very young and novice players right the way up to professional level.

I would suggest you study one technique at a time because I don't want you to get overwhelmed and think that soccer is overly complicated, because it's not.

In reality, the game of football is pretty basic, but you do need to understand the fundamentals in order to get a foundation from where you can develop your own skills.

You have already gained knowledge about the different positions available, plus learned the basic rules of the game and how they are applied.

Now it's time to look at the basic plays so as to understand just how the game is performed.

Let us start with the first movement which is the wall pass.

This is the most basic soccer play and no doubt one of the first things that beginners will learn when they come into contact with the game.

The Wall Pass

The wall pass is also known as the give and go and the one-two.

It is the most frequently used method of play in soccer and that's because it's so efficient, whether playing backyard soccer or in a competition final.

It's highly effective when you want to get rid of an opponent quickly without needing to challenge him in a dribbling duel.

It is done by quickly passing the ball to the nearest standing teammate, followed by a quick run around the opponent, and then receiving the ball back (see illustration).

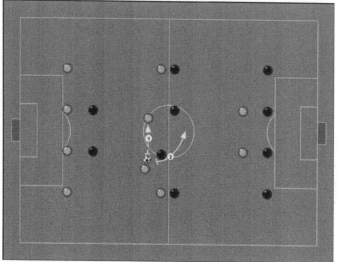

There are two key aspects when it comes to the wall pass, as follows:

1. Your teammate is supposed to pass the ball back after one touch. It is therefore important to have him understand what your intentions are to avoid any cock-ups.

2. Speed is of the essence! Smarter and more skillful opponents are often aware what is about to happen. This means it is really important to perform the wall pass as quickly as possible in order to pull it off successfully.

While the wall pass is often associated with offensive tactics, it can also be easily utilized in defense as well. You've probably seen it countless times when watching professional soccer LIVE or on TV.

For example, a common situation when the wall pass is used in defense is when a defender finds himself under great pressure while in possession of the ball.

Instead of clearing the ball away, he would play himself out of the pressured situation with a wall pass and therefore still get to keep the ball under his control.

So next time you watch soccer, make sure to pay close attention to the wall pass and you will notice just how simple and powerful it is.

Running into Free Space

Running into free space requires great pace and skill. This is a method that actually has much in common with the wall pass (outlined in the previous chapter), but there is a difference. Here you are forcing your opponent to follow along and therefore leave his position.

The run itself is usually between 10-20 yards, depending on how hard the pass is. In general, the player running into the free space will need to catch up with the ball as it will usually be passed at high speed.

Running into free space is a great way to cause problems in the other team's defense.

This is because one or more opponents will be forced to chase the player who is running into the free space, and this consequently leaves huge gaps in their defense.

By utilizing this skill properly, you will also open up opportunities to play the ball in the opposite direction. This is achieved because a player can easily make a run into free space without actually receiving the ball back.

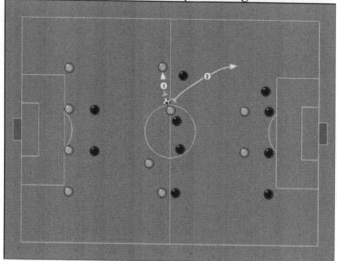

The run should be performed at maximum speed in order to force the opponent to follow, thus pulling apart their defense by creating holes in it.

As you can see, this is an approach where having good stamina and the ability to follow through is crucial.

It is also worth noting that in a soccer game you will often only have the ball at your feet for around two minutes per match.

That means the remaining 88 minutes will be spent running into free space, marking opponents, and being available for passes, even though you may never actually get the ball.

Through Pass – Slicing Through Defense

A through pass is a method of play used to slice through the opponent's defense with a single forward pass.

It can be the ideal weapon for beating a defense that likes to play higher up in the field, as this leaves bigger gaps behind them.

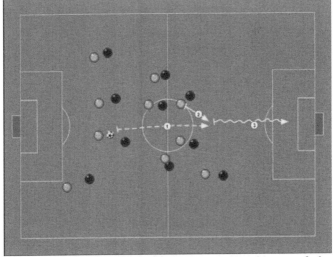

The moment a through pass is played one of the strikers should have already started his run into position.

However, he needs to time his run carefully because if he starts too early he can easily be caught in an offside trap.

This is the part of a through pass where most strikers mess up things.

Even if the through pass is played at the right time, strikers can either find themselves standing in offside, or unable to avoid getting caught in it.

Although it may look simple enough in the illustration below, I can guarantee that it requires great skill if it's to be performed with any real success.

The most difficult part of the through pass is to actually kick the soccer ball with enough power so that the striker is able to meet it, get it under his control, and then continue his run towards the goal.

More skillful and experienced goalkeepers are often able to interpret what is about to happen. When they do, they will often move a few yards up the field and try to interrupt any attempts to pass through the defense.

To summarize; the through pass can be really effective for beating defense with a single move.

But as mentioned previously, it does require the player in possession of the ball, and the striker, to be completely synchronized on the field.

Target Player – The Taller the Better

The role of a target player is actually quite straightforward, and usually adopted when there are two strikers where one is taller than the other.

It is an efficient way of gaining advantage on the field and to approach the opponent's goal quickly.

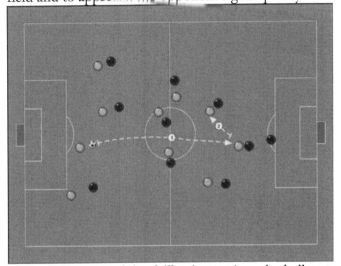

Basically, one of the fullbacks receives the ball, gets it under his control, and then performs a cross to the tallest striker.

As the ball approaches the striker, he either receives it or plays it directly on the first touch to the shorter striker, providing he is in position just a few yards away.

When the shorter striker receives the ball, he usually does one of the following:

-   Passes the ball at the flank to one of the wingers and then approaches the penalty area while waiting for the winger to play the ball inside the box.
-   Challenge the defender with a dribbling attempt, and providing he gets past him, finishes the attack with a shot at the goal.

- Gets the ball under control and then finishes the attack with a quick and well-aimed shot at the goal.
- Plays the ball backwards because of the high concentration of opponents putting pressure on him.

The most important part of this play is that the cross arrives at the head level because the target player needs to be able to safely pass it back to the shorter striker. If the fullback lacks accuracy when crossing the ball, this move is doomed to fail.

In brief, a good target player is one who is generally tall, possesses good ball control, and is able to hold off opponents and bring other teammates into play.

Counter Attack – The Art of Striking Back

The counter attack has proven to be the most effective method for scoring goals in modern day soccer. It occurs when the attacking team loses possession of the ball whilst the other team re-instates the attack.

The main reason why the counter attack is so effective is because the side that loses possession of the ball has the entire team moving forward.

This means that most players will not be on their starting positions thus causing huge gaps in their defense.

A counter-attack has to be a quick strike into the opposition half by the defending team. It really does come down to speed.

If a counter attack takes too long, the opposing team gets time to reorganize themselves, and once they do that, the counter attack is essentially over.

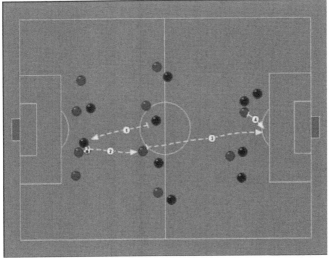

To demonstrate how a counter attack works in practice, take a look at the illustration above.

As you can see, the blue team is attacking while the red team is defending. The midfielder of the blue team has passed the ball (line 1) to the striker.

However, the fullback (line 2) of the red team has seen through his attempt and consequently regained possession of the ball and played it to the midfield.

The central midfielder of the red team (line 3) passes the ball quickly to the striker (line 4).

The striker can then either challenge the fullback of the blue team in a dribbling duel, or run past him and attempt to finish the counter attack.

Although this sounds easy in theory, it's actually much more difficult to pull off in practice.

A successful counter attack requires quick decision making and an ability to pass the ball with accuracy and determination.

Timing is everything here. The faster a team can move the ball up the field, the better their chances are of scoring.

To summarize this chapter, a successful counter-attack can beat even the most experienced, skillful, and well-oiled defense. There is no team in the world that is able to defend themselves from a well-organized counter attack.

Set Plays - Increased Scoring by 40%

The expression "set play" is used in soccer to refer to a situation where the ball is returned to open play following a stoppage.

According to studies done on set plays, a team can actually increase their scoring potential by up to 40% by taking advantage of them.

There are numerous circumstances where set plays can occur and they can each be modified into various different forms.

So as to avoid complicating things, it's best to think of a set play as a combination of one or several methods of play.

Set plays are opportunities that can be provided by corner kicks, free kicks, and indirect kicks. You might be surprised to know that over one third of all goals in professional games are scored as a direct result of set play opportunities.

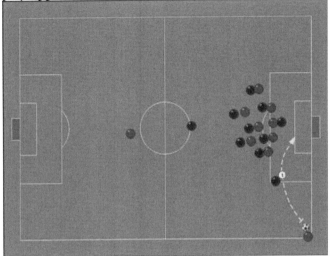

When exploited properly, a set play can confuse the opponents and pull them apart to create spaces in their defense; something which increases the scoring potential.

Most coaches will spend some training sessions practicing the various set plays. This is necessary if the team is to become familiar and comfortable with them as and when the opportunities arise.

Personally, I think that amateur players should only be given a maximum of three set plays per game. For example, one could be for the corner kick, another for an indirect free kick, and finally one for a free kick.

Furthermore, these set plays should not have more than two different runs.

If there are more than three set plays per match, then there's always a risk of players becoming confused and disorientated with the game.

In the illustration above, I have given a basic example of a set play involving a corner. In this case, one of the players is supposed to run at the first post while the other one moves away in order to create the necessary space to run into.

Although this set play is a pretty simple example, it could easily be modified further by introducing different combinations of runs.

Just remember, the more runs involved in a specific type of set play, the harder it will be for the players to recall and coordinate what it is they are supposed to be doing during the corners and free kicks.

Ending...

My final piece of advice to you is as follows: If you have a dream, do not give up on it even if someone you look up to says you can't do it. Remember to always, always, always believe in yourself. If you don't, then those who you need to, won't believe in you either! Be mindful of the fact that there is only one real failure in this life of ours, and that is the failure to try. Best of luck in all your endeavors. Mirsad Hasic

24681249R00057

Made in the USA
Middletown, DE
02 October 2015